NLP AND DARK

PSYCHOLOGY

*9+1 NLP Techniques for Beginners
and Advanced to Manipulate People
by Improving Your Art of
Persuasion and Body Language*

Table of Contents

Introduction

There are a lot of great things about NLP, but many people have a lot of misconceptions that come with NLP. Some people, even within the field of psychology, are against NLP and think that it is a bad thing. They worry that this tool, when put into the wrong hands, could end up causing more damage than good, even if it does end up benefiting the one who learns how to use it.

This book contains proven steps and strategies on how to apply Neuro-Linguistic Programming in all areas of your daily life. It also explains what Neuro-Linguistic Programming is, who can use it, when to use it, its benefits, principles, techniques, and application to different areas of your day-to-day life. This system will improve the way that you perceive the world and give you a wider perspective.

Although Neuro-Linguistic Programming may sound very complex, it's easier to incorporate into your life than you may think. With the aid of this guide, even the beginner can understand the principles and apply them to the way that everyday decisions are made. This can enhance life and give learners a much wider geographical perspective, thus enriching their lives. When these techniques are employed, they open up a whole new way of thinking.

With NLP, you can upgrade your mindset. You can make your memory better, have better communication skills, your intelligence quotient will most likely rank higher the next time you take the test among other skills that you can improve, modify and enhance either on yourself or on someone else.

The following chapters will discuss how to use neuro-linguistic programming and dark psychology techniques to manipulate people and get everything that you want out of them.

NLP is something that helps you to learn more about the people around you. It helps you to learn how to read the body language of those near you, and to get what you want. Any tool, when put in the wrong hands, can be dangerous. But NLP is an effective tool that can do a lot of good, especially for the one who knows how to use it.

It focuses on the practical NLP methods and techniques for persuasion, negotiation, mind control, and manipulation, along with tips to help you understand and avoid dark psychology tactics. It provides simple, straightforward NLP techniques for self-development and enhancement of your skills in dealing with the people around you, as well as aids to create a positive and meaningful environment.

The techniques can be used to better business skills, improve interpersonal skills, and discover the formula to live your life your way while striking a balance with the ethics, morals, and principles that you have set for yourself.

This guidebook is going to take some time to explore NLP and all of the parts that come with it. Inside, we are going to explore what NLP is, some of the controversies that come with NLP, and how you need to learn a bit of self-mastery before you stand a chance of learning how to use some of the tools of NLP on other people.

There are so many great benefits that can come from using NLP in your own life. It allows you to learn how to work with other people, how to read what other people are thinking and meaning, and ensures that you are able to get more of what you want and need out of life. When you are ready to learn more about NLP, especially dark NLP, and how to use it in your own life, make sure to check out this guidebook to help you get started.

Chapter 1: What Is NLP and How Does It Work?

NLP stands for Neuro-linguistic Programming and focuses on the language your mind speaks and how it functions. To use an example, have you ever tried to hold a conversation with someone that didn't speak the same language as you? The common picture painted is a couple going out to a fancy French restaurant. You read the menu and believe you'd ordered a soup, but instead, you're treated to a plate of liver and onions.

This scene can be used to explain what goes on within our own unconscious mind. We look at the menu and believe we've put in our order for a well-paying job, a nice house, a fulfilling relationship, a happy family, and toned abs, but if that's not what ended up, then there's been some sort of miscommunication along the way. Within NLP, it's often said that your unconscious mind is the part that sets your goals, while your conscious mind is the part that accomplishes those goals. Your unconscious mind holds your deepest desires, and the truth about what you want in life, but if you don't know how to communicate this properly, then you'll always end up with the wrong menu item.

Take a common vice such as procrastination and understand your unconscious mind only acts this way because it's led to believe that's what you desire. Understanding and studying NLP is like taking that French language course, so you're able to tell the waiter, who is your unconscious mind, what you truly want out of your life. Unless you're able to communicate successfully, you won't be able to match your unconscious and conscious minds together.

NLP is a powerful tool and technique used to speak with yourself, to overcome challenges within your life. These challenges can include fears and phobias, different beliefs, and various other roadblocks created by your mind. Not only does understanding NLP make you a better communicator with yourself, but it also assists you in communicating with others. You'll be able to influence other people in your life in positive ways, so that they could possibly overcome their own fears within their lives. This will also help to better their own lives.

NLP was founded by two different men by studying different therapies and focusing on modeling. They watched and observed others, breaking down the language they would use and the ability to produce a change in others. If there is a result that you would like to duplicate, you can produce the same result by breaking down the interaction. This consists of modeling different

17

language patterns, how someone takes in information and processes it. If a successful person can accomplish amazing feats, then copying their methods should allow you to be just as successful.

We process information in multiple different ways, and a large part of NLP relies on the understanding that so that we can change it. We want to change our view on certain information, whether that be positive or negative. We also tie certain emotions and moments together that can be shifted. Numerous people have used NLP to become a more motivated person in their everyday life, and to be happy overall. Now that we've homed in on what NLP is, we'll give you a few tricks to make it work for you. Before we begin, let's start by saying this is only some quick tricks to help you understand and use NLP to help better your life. In order to get the full extent of NLP information, we'd need an entire book, if not multiple books, to dive that far into it. However, these methods are simple and can help you as fast as you begin to use them.

The only thing that matters within NLP is the truths you hold within yourself; another person's perception means almost nothing. Someone can tell you that your outfit looks gross, and they are operating off their own definition. However, that doesn't mean that your definition must be the exact same; it only matters what you believe. You hold all the power within your belief, and that belief shapes your reality. Believing that your outfit makes you look like a model better serves you in your life and it'll benefit you to believe as such. This is the only bit of information that is useful to you and your life.

NLP also uses certain methods that help you break habits. Let's say that there's an action like smoking cigarettes or something you do a lot that you want to stop doing, you'd explore the Swish pattern.

Despite coming up with a plan to stop smoking, and being motivated at that moment, you end up not following through. Instead, you forget the plan you've created and gone right back to lighting up another. The Swish pattern takes that idea of starting a program, like a journey to stop smoking, and gives it a new view. When you're creating a plan, you tend to think about the experience of trying to quit smoking, instead of visualizing yourself within that experience. On the opposite side, this is the root of trauma and triggers within your life, because people will snap back to that experience as if they are there. It gives you the urge to begin to panic and to act out of pure fear, instead of realizing the new situation at hand. The exact same thing happens when you form a plan to break a habit.

You continually break your plan and fall back into the feeling of disappointment and failure. You replace the image you continually have of failing

20

in your goals, and you swish it with an image of yourself. Instead of seeing your failures, you see yourself as you want to be. This is powerful because most people cannot visualize the outcome and can only see the problem in front of their face.

The swish method allows you to visualize yourself as a non-smoker and to live a happy and healthy life, on the other side of your program.

This is tremendously motivating and gives you a mental image to work towards instead of simply saying you need to quit your bad habits.

If you're only focused on not smoking so much, then you're focusing on smoking, which makes you want to smoke more. Use that mental image of yourself and keep it vague, so you can associate that image with a relatable future you. You can always swish an image of you denying a cigarette or not smoking, and it may work sometimes, but won't work all the time. Visualize yourself as a better you, overall, and you'll find the effects to be amazingly beneficial when it comes to breaking habits.

Visualizing is a powerful tool within NLP if you're feeling unmotivated, depressed, or procrastinating on something that you need to be done. Studies show that when we think of something we enjoy doing and close our eyes, we tend to view that item or action as close, vibrant, large. If you enjoy playing basketball, the visual of a basketball will be bright within your mind. In order to create motivation, you need to use this same idea, but in reverse, by bringing an image closer to you. Close your eyes and try visualizing that item or that action in your mind. Odds are, it seems far away and dimly lit, because you believe it to be out of your reach. Every person visualizes within their mind, whether they think, they do or not. Take the image of that action that you don't enjoy doing and visualize it in your mind. Picture the image brighter, bigger, and more within your reach and control. It may seem silly, but practicing this technique over time will change the way you view the undesired action. No longer will you become depressed at the thought or procrastinate because it feels much more within reach.

Some people rely more on auditory than on visual. However, this works almost the exact same way. When you close your eyes and think about something you hate, what kind of dialogue do you have with yourself? This dialogue can reference your inner dialogue, as well as outer. What kinds of things do you say about it? Now, imagine something you enjoy doing, and compare the two. Typically, your facial expression may even spread into a smile. For example, say you're trying to motivate yourself to clean your kitchen. Try speaking similarly to yourself when thinking of cleaning your kitchen. Change your tone, tell yourself that you enjoy it, and use empowering language. This will change any negative feeling you have to a positive one.

Another positive technique of NLP we'll cover is known as "Anchoring." Anchoring is the process of tying an emotion with an action on the concept, so that you feel that emotion whenever you activate it. For instance, if you're driving in your car and see an ambulance behind you with its lights turned on. It's normal to feel a sense of dread or to feel stressed out.

If you see the lights and hear the siren again even if it's not attached to an ambulance, you'll feel the same sense of dread you had before. The image of that ambulance is anchored to that emotion. Take an example of homework and the feelings you get when looking at an unfinished page.

Those emotions have been tied to that image your entire life. This is also how advertisements take hold of your attention and incite emotion within you.

Commercials with happy family gatherings may make you feel elated, and then the product flashes, allowing you to anchor that elation to the product they're trying to sell.

Using this same logic to assist us can be incredibly beneficial. While you're in the midst of a happy experience, such as an event with friends, or maybe even a concert, start doing something such as snapping your fingers or clapping your hands. Choose an action that you don't do so often, it needs to be unique. When you begin to feel sad or unmotivated, begin to clap your hands or snap your fingers to incite that same emotion. Just as you can create a positive anchor, there are also such things as a negative anchor. Often, people can't get any work done within their bedrooms because of the anchor they've created. You get inside your bed when it's time to sleep, and thus, an anchor is created for sleep. Possibly, your room is where you retreat when you're feeling depressed, so you create a negative anchor for being depressed. The trick is to notice these occurrences and avoid the negative anchors while inciting positive ones.

"Reframing" is also a proven helpful technique within the realm of NLP. Imagine that every moment of your life has a picture snapped of it and put into a single frame.

You feel a certain way when you look at the picture and recall that moment in your life. Reframing speaks of taking a hold of that photo and turning it to the side to get a brand-new view of it.

Before long, you're looking at the photo like you never have before, and what really matters, you've changed how you feel about that moment, as well. For example, there's a moment in your life when you got in trouble for having bad grades in school. Possibly, you walked away from that moment feeling like you were a bad person, and that you weren't good enough to get better grades in school. Try turning the frame and giving this moment in your life some new perspective. Instead of looking at it with a negative view, think of the positives.

Try to get a grasp on how that moment made you stronger, and what you took forward with you to better your life. Instead, view that moment of your life through a better lens and think about how it made you work harder in school and then in your work life once you graduated.

Did it always help to launch you over the line of expectations? Instead of using negative experiences, turn them into positive ones. You could blame your parents, blame your teacher, blame your school, or you could learn from the responsibility and grow.

This technique also teaches you to be grateful for moments that you felt uncomfortable or that you previously viewed with a different setting.

Reframing also works with conversations and miscommunication. Often, we react to the way we perceive a situation or a conversation, only to find out later that we've misrepresented it. Take control of how you feel about moments in your life, and make sure you aren't looking back with regret.

A common NLP method that can be used by anyone and everyone is mirroring. You read a version of this within our persuasion techniques chapter, but mirroring someone firmly falls within the belief of NLP. Mirroring someone's movements creates a sense of friendship, and you become vastly more comfortable with someone who is performing the same movements as you. Without realizing it, you let your guard down, and you begin to connect with the person that is mimicking you. In this way, you can easily build rapport with someone a quick way. Once you've built rapport with someone, you'll find that it's easy to lead their emotions with yours. If you have someone that is speaking quietly and a little more reserved, once you've mirrored them and caught their interest, if you speed up your talking, you'll find the other person is doing the same. You can also perform the opposite or take it in a completely different direction. Either way, you've built rapport and can now build from there.

NLP, in a nutshell, seeks to better your mental health and trick yourself into becoming someone who gets things done. One of the negatives that people say of NLP is that it can be used in an evil way, but it all comes down to what your intentions are.

If you're doing it to lie or deceit, to manipulate someone into liking you, and the like, then you could be venturing down a dangerous path. Everyone wishes to be influenced in some way, whether by a movie or this book. In a way, these pages are influencing you, but in an incredibly positive way.

How to Use Neuro-Linguistic Programming (NLP)

The most fundamental, basic principle of NLP is positive language. No, I'm not suggesting that by keeping a stiff upper lip, you might be able to ignore all of your problems — rather, this approach is based on science. You see, the brain is incapable of processing negative language. This means that if you were to tell your communicative partner, "Please do not touch me," what their subconscious mind would be hearing is, "Please do touch me."

According to NLP, your subconscious mind regulates everything from digestion to breathing. This suggests that you are able to communicate with your own subconscious using this technique, as well. The idea is that if you were to repeat, "Do not get well," to yourself as a mantra, your subconscious would only hear, "Do get well," and would respond to this. Of course, negative language is best used in this way on others, and not yourself, because it's entirely possible to just repeat positive mantras to yourself. Many people are unaware of the fact that the subconscious mind is incapable of hearing negative speech (such as 'no' or 'can't'), which makes it even easier to covertly implant ideas into their subconscious minds without them even being aware that you are the one willing them to act in a certain way.

The only time during which you have to be cognizant of your own internal dialogue when considering the effect of negative language on the subconscious mind is when your self-talk begins using negatives without your awareness. For example, if you accidentally think, "I hope I don't get nervous during this interview," your subconscious mind will hear, "I hope I do get nervous during this interview." For this reason, it is incredibly important to be mindful of the tone of your own internal dialogue, and phrase thoughts positively like, "I hope I am calm during the interview," to bypass negative speech impact on your brain.

The second most fundamental principle of using NLP is targeted talk. NLP theorizes that all people communicate in one of three ways: auditory, visual, or kinesthetic. Furthermore, NLP demands of its users to be aware of these communicative styles and to try to pinpoint which best suits their communicative partner. When your words fit your unique communicative style, it is much easier to deliver new ideas into someone's mind.

The best way to find out someone's communicative style is through listening to them speak. Someone whose style can be described as auditory might use phrases such as: "That sounds great" or "I hear you're busy working on a project". Those who are more prone to kinesthetic communication might say something like "This homework is hard" or "I feel like you are not listening to me" or even, "I'm going through a rough time". Those who are visual communicators, on the other hand, use phrases like "I see you went to the shops again this morning" or "Look on the bright side".

Once you determine the style which best fits your communicative partner, you can start using this to your advantage. Visual people are more likely to be complacent if you communicate with them using gestures and smiles. Another great suggestion is to employ vivid, descriptive language to express any physical places or things visually. It is a good idea to do this if you would like to draw your communicative partner in and keep them focused on you.

Auditory people listen to a speaker's tone and intonation. It is thus very important to control the pitch and sound of your voice, using inflections and variances in both to keep your communicative partner engaged.

Kinesthetic learners are 'feelers' and not 'thinkers'. If you can tap into this by using emotive language, instead of just delivering the facts, you're far more likely to be successful in your communication with them. Furthermore, telling them "I have a gut feeling about this", might make them more prone to believe you, as this is the level at which they operate.

Of course, learning what your communicative partner's communicative style is can take some time, as you would essentially need to build a rapport with them first. Luckily, there is a way to bypass this that is nearly as effective as observing someone's patterns of speech. The trick is to watch their eyes.

Kinesthetic thinkers tend to look down while they are communicating, whilst auditory thinkers laterally left or right and visual thinkers look up and straight ahead. Watching someone's eye movements might reveal an incredible amount about how they choose to communicate and how best to communicate with them.

The next NLP technique, which is easy to use and very effective, is known as mirroring. The mirroring technique is based on the idea that we are more prone to trusting people who share similarities with us, such as mannerisms and speech patterns. This means that through careful observation, one might be able to imbibe a few of another person's characteristics. This will eventually help them trust you and share similar perspectives.

The trick with mirroring is not to make it too obvious. If you simply copy your communicative partner's behavior, they'll soon become suspicious and wonder what you are up to. The best way to mirror someone is by matching their speech patterns covertly. If someone is very prone to using slang in their speech, it might be a good idea, for example, to throw some slang words into your own communications with them. Speech isn't the only thing that can be mirrored, though.

Gestures are a good place to start. For example, if your communicative partner is sitting with their legs crossed, you may want to do the same. Here too, you will need to employ a measure of stealth and not mimic every gesture they make.

Disassociation is another NLP technique that is often used by practitioners. Disassociation cannot usually be used on a communicative partner; instead, its purpose is to help the user overcome negative emotions. These are the steps to follow to employ disassociation:

Identify how you are feeling. Are you feeling sad? Angry? Frustrated? Perhaps scared?

Once you have identified the feeling that you are experiencing, imagine yourself floating out of your body, exiting from the top of your head. Imagine yourself looking down at your body and seeing its surroundings and how it is reacting to the negative emotion you wish to eliminate.

Finally, imagine the feeling within yourself changing. Perhaps, you feel your chest tightening from nervousness — now imagine feeling that knot in your chest slowly unravel and become loose and comfortable.

Anchoring is the next technique, and this one can be used on communicative partners. Anchoring originated from Ivan Pavlov's theory of classical conditioning. Pavlov conducted an experiment in which he would ring a bell whenever his dogs were eating. After a period, Pavlov was able to get the dogs to salivate just by ringing the bell, even when there was no food present. Anchoring works in much the same way.

When using anchoring on a communicative partner, start off by conditioning them with a certain gesture or phrase. Whenever they're experiencing the emotion you would like to elicit in the future, employ this gesture or phrase to connect these two experiences in your communicative partner's mind. If you have been successful in creating an 'anchor,' you should be able to elicit this emotion within your communicative partner simply by using the phrase or gesture in front of them, without any outside stimuli or manipulation.

Another very useful technique is called the "concealed commands" method. A concealed command is a manner of phrasing a question in such a way that your communicative partner does not realize that you are directing him or her toward a set outcome. An example of a concealed command is, "Which movie would you like to watch?" instead of asking, "Would you like to watch a movie?"

The "if you want" technique is somewhat similar to the "concealed commands" method in that they both rely heavily on wordplay. The purpose of the "if you want" technique is to get your communicative partner to do something that you do not want to do. An example of this is asking your communicative partner, "I can pay the bill if you want" – your communicative partner will feel that since you've offered to pay the bill, etiquette demands they now make the same offer. Which, of course, you will accept. In this way, you're actually shifting the responsibility for the problem onto your communicative partner and away from yourself.

However, wordplay in NLP doesn't just end and begin with concealed commands and the "if you want" technique. NLP also emphasizes the importance of the word 'but.' 'But' is a special word because the human mind generally only hears and focuses on the part of the sentence after the 'but.' For example, if I said, "Susan is a pretty girl but she has horrible teeth", all that my communicative partner would hear is that Susan has horrible teeth. If I reworded the question as, "Susan has horrible teeth, but she is a pretty girl", all that my communicative partner's mind would absorb is that Susan is a pretty girl.

The opposite is true for the word 'and.' The human mind only hears whatever part of the sentence came before 'and.' This means that if I were to say, "We are going swimming and then we will have lunch," the only thing our mind would focus on is that we are going swimming. However, if I rephrased the sentence to say, "We are going to have lunch, and before that we will go swimming," all the mind would hear is that we are going to have lunch.

Words aren't the only things that hold power in NLP, though. Touch is also important. When

41

you're building a rapport (establishing the trust) with a new communicative partner, a few well-placed touches on the upper arm during conversation can lead them into feeling a sense of trust toward you sooner rather than later.

The final NLP technique to be aware of is pacing. Essentially, pacing requires that you give, for example, three definite facts to your communicative partner, followed by the concept that you want your communicative partner to accept as the truth. An example of a pacing script is the following: "Our boss is on leave today (first true fact), and she took the secretaries with her (second true fact). The chief executive officer is here, though (third true fact). Our boss is always on leave (untrue fact)." Because you've prefaced the untrue fact (that your boss is always on leave) by first giving two or three definite facts, your communicative partner is more likely to accept the untrue fact as absolute truth.

Uses of NLP

NLP has many uses and dark manipulation is not on the top of the list. As a matter of fact, NLP is used for personal growth and self-improvement. If you want to become a better version of yourself, you can use some of the techniques above to reprogram your mind. Through visualization, you can easily change your negative perceptions of life and start observing it in a positive way. It is important to note that NLP is designed for self-growth and can help you restore your self-esteem and improve your thinking process.

NLP is used to promote skills such as self-reflection, communication, and confidence, among others. You can use NLP to achieve work-oriented goals and see success in your relationships with others. If you implement the techniques right, you will gather influence as a leader and easily rise to a position of power within your work environment.

With that said, it is also relevant to mention the dark side of NLP. The fact that the language can lead to a total reprogramming of a person's mind is a big risk. The fact that through NLP, you can learn about a person's beliefs and be able to influence them makes it a dangerous tool. If you want to practice NLP, you should have the intention to progress. Your main target should be growth and improved productivity. You must reduce your selfish ambitions and focus on the common good of the majority. You can use NLP to help the individuals you work with or the people who work under you realize their full potential. You can also use NLP to improve your personal performance and your socialization with other people within your firm.

NLP is also applied in medical terms, especially when dealing with mental conditions. It can be used to help individuals suffering from anxiety and depression. Most of those individuals only experience worry, fear, and panic attacks because some situations trigger past events. Through the NLP approach, you can help those individuals change their emotional associations. You can help them start associating certain circumstances with positive and not negative reactions. The sensory association on certain triggers may help patients of anxiety and depression improve their general outlook on life.

NLP has also been found to be helpful for PTSD patients. Any person that has gone through traumatic events in life may have a very unrealistic approach to life. Negativity becomes a constant part of the life of those individuals. If you learn to use NLP, you can bond with those individuals, extract the right information, and use it to reprogram the minds of the people you are targeting.

Chapter 2: Dark psychology and NLP, How Are They Connected to Each Other?

Neuro-linguistic Programming, or NLP, has become a popular way of talking about human thought and communication for many non-psychologists. It's a version of Popular Psychology. While it's far beyond the reach of our discussion to criticize NLP (because such criticism would cover several issues), you must know a few things about the communication and non-verbal skills and strategies. That is supposed to be efficient and being promoted by both reputable and untrustworthy teachers and so-called master practitioners. Unlike mainstream or popular areas such as linguistics, neuroscience, or psychology, which have their basis in academic research using controlled studies, NLP tends to focus on "what works" and derives many of its methods from other disciplines in practice. So, while several non-verbal communication NLP methods and declarations may have strong research support, it is also likely that some of the techniques and arguments are not validated correctly in controlled study environments.

The message for casual non-verbal communication students is that reading NLP content may introduce you to some excellent and right concepts from fields such as psychology and linguistics. Still, it will also expose you to ideas and assumptions that are not validated or may be invalid. The problem is that you are not going to be able to assess what is valid and what isn't by relying on NLP literature and courses. NLP does not provide a unified theory — it's more of a hodge-podge of useful things.

To make things worse, NLP relies heavily on ads and arguments, unlike more scientific science-based disciplines, and has attracted inexperienced people or people with dubious motives. And, who could be called New Age practitioners respectfully?

To explain the range of things that some practitioners include in NLP: the principle or principles are borrowed from linguistics, certainly a valid and agreed way of looking at communication. On the other extreme is the hypnotic regression of past life, which is far outside the limits of accepted scientific practice. Both are deemed part of the NLP. Then, to clarify, marketing claims and professionals who say they can show you how to tell you when people are lying by looking at their eye movements and how to seduce women by applying NLP techniques can be found.

All this to explain why we don't have non-verbal behavioral elements that are explicitly taken from NLP and not present in more traditional, well-researched, and regulated fields. In this topic, you will find that many things discussed ARE part of NLP, but they are included because they were developed before or outside the NLP community.

The concept found within the NLP is that professional communicators use standard verbal and non-verbal communication techniques to establish interaction with others. Such approaches are based on an understanding of the internal sensory interpretation structures that are used by people to interpret and make sense of their experiences. An in-depth NLP Training will try to ensure that you gain a highly evolved ability to recognize this very subtle form of communication and respond to it. That's because it is one of the necessary skills that much of the 'magic' of NLP depends upon. Applying NLP to communicate

49

expertly, develop excellent relations, or coaching someone in personal development, or using most of the well-known NLP techniques requires you to have a unique ability to recognize non-verbal communication.

NLP is a lot like a user manual for the brain, to help you communicate the goals and desires of the unconscious mind to the conscious self. Imagine you are in a foreign country and craving chicken wings, so you go to a restaurant to order the same, but when the food shows up, it ends up being liver stew because of a failed communication.

Humans often fail to recognize and acknowledge their unconscious thoughts and desires because a lot of it gets lost in translation to the conscious self. NLP enthusiasts often exclaim, "The conscious mind is the goal setter, and the unconscious mind is the goal-getter".

The idea being your unconscious mind wants you to achieve everything that you actually desire, but if your conscious mind fails to receive the message, you will never set the goal to achieve those dreams.

NLP was developed using excellent therapists and communicators who had achieved great success as role models. It's a set of tools and techniques to help your master communication, both with yourself and others.

NLP is the study of the human mind combining thoughts and actions with perception to fulfil their deepest desires. Our mind employs complex neural networks to process information and use language or auditory signals to give it meaning while storing these signals in patterns to generate and store new memories.

We can voluntarily use and apply certain tools and techniques to alter our thoughts and actions in achieving our goals. These techniques can be perceptual, behavioral, and communicative and used to control our own mind as well as that of others.

One of the central ideas of NLP is that our conscious mind has a bias towards a specific sensory system called the "Preferred Representational System (PRS)." Phrases like, "I hear you" or "Sounds good" signal an auditory PRS, whereas the phrase like, "I see you" may signal a visual PRS.

A certified therapist can identify a person's PRS and model their therapeutic treatment around it. This therapeutic framework often involves rapport building, goal setting, and information gathering, among other activities.

NLP is increasingly used by individuals to promote self-enhancement, such as self-reflection and confidence as well as for social skill development, primarily communication.

NLP therapy or training can be delivered in the form of language and sensory-based interventions, using behavior modification techniques customized for individuals to better their social communication and improved confidence and self-awareness.

NLP therapists or trainers strive to make their client understand that their view and perception of the world is directly associated with how they operate in it, and the first step toward a better future is the keen understanding of their conscious self and contact with their unconscious mind.

It's paramount to first analysis and subsequently change our thoughts and behaviors that are counterproductive and block our success and healing. NLP has been successfully used in the treatment of various mental health conditions like anxiety, phobias, stress, and even post-traumatic stress disorder.

An increasing number of practitioners are commercially applying NLP to promise improved productivity and achievement of work-oriented goals that ultimately lead to job progression.

Now, let's look at how NLP works. John Grinder, in association with his student Richard Bandler, conducted a research study on techniques used by Fritz Perls (founder of Gestalt therapy), Virginia Satir (Family therapist), and Milton Erickson (renowned Hypnotherapist). They subsequently analyzed and streamlined these therapy techniques to create a behavioral model for mass application in order to achieve and reproduce excellence in any field. Bandler, a computer science major, helped develop a "psychological programming language" for human beings.

On the basis of how our mind processes information or perceives the external world, it generates an internal "NLP map" of what is going on outside. This internal map is created based on the feedback provided by our sense organs, like the pictures we take in, sounds we hear, the taste in our mouth, sensations we feel on our skin, and what we can smell.

However, with this massive influx of information, our mind selectively deletes and generalizes a ton of information. This selection is unique to every person and is determined by what our mind deems relevant to our situation.

As a result, we often miss out on a whole lot of information that can be immediately noticed by someone else right off the bat, and we end up with a tiny and skewed version of what is really occurring. For example, take a moment and process this statement: "Person A killed person B," now depending on our circumstances and experiences, we will all have our own version of that story.

Some might think an "a man killed a woman," or "a lion killed a man" or "a terrorist killed a baby" or "John Doe killed Kennedy" and so on and so forth.

Now, there's a method to this madness, whatever story you came up with, realize there is a way you got to that story which was driven by our own life experience.

Our mind creates an internal map of the situation at hand, and then we compare that map with other internal maps from our past that we have stored in our minds. Every person has their own internal "library" based on what is important or relevant to them in accordance with their personality.

Did you ever feel that once your conscious mind makes you aware of what you want to do or gain, suddenly, the universe seems to be propping up signs that could help you find your way to get what you want? For example, one day you wake up thinking, I need to take my family on vacation.

You go on with your day the same way as you have been for days or weeks, but you suddenly notice a poster on an exciting trip to Florida on your way to work, that you later learnt from your coworker has been up for over a month now. You suddenly see that close to the same Starbucks that you visit every day, there is a big travel agency that you had never paid attention.

When browsing the Internet, you will suddenly see travel ads all over your Facebook or ads from

Airbnb popping up on your YouTube videos. Now all these may come across as coincidences, but the matter of the fact is those things or signs had been there all along, but your mind deleted that information or perception because they were not relevant to you.

So as your conscious mind starts connecting the dots between your wishes and the reality of the world, you start picking up on new information that may have already been in plain sight, but you are only tuned into now.

What Is Dark NLP?

Your personality profile also plays a major role in what information your mind chooses to exclude and what is processed. People who are more focused on security, they are constantly assessing their situation to determine whether it is safe for you or not.

On the other hand, people who are more freedom-oriented, they tend to think of their situation in terms of options and limitation with no focus on safety at all.

Your personality determines what and how you update your mental library and, ultimately, the meaning you add to these internal maps. For example, a kid looking at a roller coaster is thinking only about the fun of traveling through open space in a cool looking ride and, given the opportunity, will easily and fearlessly jump on the ride because his personality is not security-oriented.

But an adult who is able to focus not only on the fun and excitement of the ride but also on its safety and potential hazards, will think twice before making that same decision.

Here are some prominently used NLP techniques:

Anchoring

A Russian scientist, Ivan Pavlov, conducted an experiment on dogs by repeatedly ringing a bell while the dogs were eating and concluded that he could get the dogs to salivate by the ringing of the bell at any time, even when there was no food present.

This neurobiological connection observed in the dogs between the bell and salivation is called a conditioned response or "anchor".

Thus, the process of creating a perceivable sensory trigger to the state of how you feel is called Anchoring.

Try this yourself! Think of a gesture or sensation on your body (pulling your earlobe, cracking your knuckles, or touching your forehead) and associate it with any desired positive emotional response (happiness, confidence, calmness, etc.)

by recalling and reliving the memory when you actually experienced those emotions.

The next time you are feeling stressed or low, you can trigger this anchor voluntarily and you will notice your feeling will immediately change. To strengthen triggered response, you can think of another memory when you felt the desired emotion and relive it.

Every time you add a new memory to the mix, your anchor will become more potent and trigger a stronger response.

Content Reframing

This NLP technique is best suited to combat negative thoughts and feelings. With the use of these visualization techniques, you can alter your mind to think differently about situations where you feel threatened or disempowered.

Simply view the negative situation and reframe it's meaning into something positive. For example, let's say you just broke up with your long-term girlfriend or boyfriend. You will most likely be hurt and in pain. But you can choose to reframe the end of your relationship with empowering thoughts of being single and new potential relationships.

You can choose to focus on the lessons you learnt from your past relationship and how you can implement them to have an even better relationship in the future. Thus, by simply reframing the break-up, you can feel better and empower yourself.

This technique has massive appeal in the treatment of post-traumatic stress disorder and for people who have experienced child abuse or are suffering from chronic or life-threatening diseases.

Rapport Building

Rapport is the art of generating empathy in others by pacing and mirroring their verbal and non-verbal behaviors. People like other people who they think are similar to themselves.

When you can subtly mirror the other person, their brain will fire off "mirror neurons" or "pleasure sensors" in their brain, which make them feel a sense of liking for you. You can simply stand or sit the way the other person or tilt your head in the same direction as theirs or the best of all, just smile when they smile. All these cues will help you build rapport with the other person. The social significance of rapport building cannot be underscored. Strong personal and professional connections lead to a happier and longer life.

Dissociation

The NLP technique of dissociation guides you to sever the link between negative emotions and the associated trigger. For instance, certain words or phrases may instantly bring back bad memories and make you feel stressed or depressed. If you can successfully identify those triggers and make an effort to detach those negative feelings from it, you are one-step closer to healing and empowering yourself.

A slew of mental health conditions like anxiety, depression, and even phobias can be effectively treated with this technique. It can also be used to deal with difficult situations at home and work positively.

Future Pacing

The NLP technique of leading the subject to a future state and rehearsing the potential future outcomes so as to achieve the desired outcome automatically is called Future Pacing. It's a type of visualization technique or mental imagery used to anchor a change or resources to future situations by imagining and virtually experiencing those situations.

A skilled manipulator can lead their victim on a mental journey into the future and influence the responses occurring when the future unfolds. An expert NLP user with prominent Dark Psychological traits may cognitively transport their victim into the future and suggest outcomes while monitoring the victim's response to get their own desired outcome into the psyche of the victim eventually.

Influence and Persuasion

This is definitely the most ambivalent NLP technique and houses a gray area between Dark Psychology and Psychotherapy.

NLP is primarily focused on eliminating negative emotions, curb bad habits, and resolve conflicts; another aspect of NLP deals with ethically influencing and persuade others. Now pay attention to the word ETHICAL here.

One of the prominent psychology therapist to participate in Grinder's original research on NLP was Milton Erickson, leading hypnotherapist and founder of the "American Society for Clinical Hypnosis". Erickson was so adept at hypnosis that he could literally hypnotize anyone anywhere and communicate with people's subconscious mind without needing hypnosis.

He helped to construct the "Milton Model" of NLP, designed to induce a trance-like state in people, using abstract language patterns. According to the Milton Model, using artfully vague and deliberately ambiguous sentences will trigger the person to search for the meaning of what they hear from their own life experiences and fill in the details subconsciously.

This powerful tool can be used to not only ethically influence and persuade people but also help people deal with some deep-seated negative emotions, overcome fears, and increase their self-awareness.

Using NLP to Manipulate

As you can see, NLP is highly potent. You can use it to influence yourself to believe new thoughts that can change up your behaviors. However, in the wrong hands, someone can do something very similar to people around them as well. Manipulators can use these techniques with ease not only to influence your thoughts but to control you as well. When you face this, you discover that ultimately, the problem lies not with the methods themselves, but rather, through the user. Manipulation itself and being able to influence and alter how other people see and think about you is not inherently dangerous or wrong. It is not inherently a problem for you to be able to influence your mind, or even the minds of others—however, the intentions matter.

Yes, with NLP you could break someone down. You could work to break their very self-esteem and confidence that make them who they are. You could create new thoughts for them that become the manner they address everything. You could make it a point to engage with other people in ways that are hurtful or harmful, or you could engage with them to make them better. Think about it—how often do you see professionals intentionally altering the thoughts of other people? They approach people differently. Think about therapists for a moment—or even NLP practitioners. NLP was designed so that people could alter thoughts but in a therapeutic process. It was created to create those alterations, and because of that, it is highly potent and highly effective. Ultimately, the best way to ensure that you can do better is to make sure that you know better. Make sure that you are aware of what you are doing so that you can prevent it from hurting other people. If you are going to use NLP, be mindful of the power that you have. If you are worried about other people manipulating you, be aware of the power that NLP has. With that knowledge, regularly consider whether the reason that you are doing something is that you want to do so, or if you are just engaging because you feel like you have to. When you get better at understanding the nuances between these, you will be able to defend yourself better. You will even be able to use NLP on your own to influence yourself as well, and there would be no problems with you doing that.

Chapter 3: How Does Body Language Affect Your Mind?

How Body Language Works

Body language is a strong medium of non-verbal communication consisting of actions of the hand and arm, body posture and actions, and facial cues and eye motions. It pinpoints to others what we are thinking, sometimes without them really understanding it.

We do much of this talking unintentionally and similarly many people sometimes perceive our non-verbal knowledge without really noticing that they are doing so. Most of us have no clue our non-verbal indications are having an effect. There are hundreds of these tiny-expressions and people are reading them, even if they only translate these references subconsciously.

Body Language Signs of Manipulation

To get their way, tricksters use various techniques, including tricky body language. As we discovered, people may create such movements as an emotional reaction to stressful events. If the person isn't in a tense environment or showing any other symptoms of anxiety, however, this specific behavior may suggest manipulation. In reality, manipulators will use this traditional pacifying to obtain support from you, actively or subconsciously, in order to manipulate your acts.

Neck and Hand Rubbing

If tricksters want to get their way, they appear to rub their palms together. You can even consider a stereotypical animated villain rubbing their palms together while they chuckle madly. This behavior, even Disney realizes as a sign of self-serving conspiring. Neck rubbing may imply the same thing that the manipulator fakes to be nervous or depressed to intimidate you into agreeing. And, by rubbing their neck, they experience some remorse for exploiting you and are neutralizing their shame. But they're exploiting you anyway.

Scratching Chin

When a trickster scratches their chin, they try to present uncertainty or low trust. Sometimes it is a trick to get them to give up and declare, "It is all right. I can do it." If you realize that a person is completely capable of doing the stuff you're thinking about and rubbing their chin, you can guarantee that they're attempting to trick you into doing something for them.

Stroking/Touching the Arm

When an individual rub or scratches his or her arms, he or she may try to manipulate you. But, of course, there are several reasons an individual might scratch their arms; they might just have a bug bite! But if you doubt that a person wants to influence you, and you find them scratching or rubbing their arms while speaking to you, you can take that as a sign of manipulation.

Tapping the Foot

Manipulators move their bodies in the same manner; they sometimes stamp their foot or do something identical, like tapping their pen. This may be an indication of impatience or frustration that they may use to convince you for giving in or performing, as they want. You are much more inclined to make a rash judgment as people tap their foot and might not necessarily be in their best interests.

Changing Body Posture

Manipulators often change their body position when attempting to control someone else. This can be an indication of distress or confusion that can be deliberately used by the trickster against you. Normally, our minds are trained to identify when a body is under stress or uncomfortable, so tricksters use these behavior patterns to impact your actions and decisions.

How to Manipulate and Regulate Your Own Body Language

Experts believe you can educate yourself to control it by becoming aware of your body language and even use it actively to make your communication much easier.

I recommend making videos and observing the video with the audio off. Use respiratory and mindfulness exercises to soothe yourself before a session so that you are more conscious of your body movement.

Altering your body language in an intentional way to better communicate with another person is also useful. The method, called mirroring, requires understanding and subtly imitating, the facial movements, body position, tone of voice, and other micro-expressions conveyed by the person you're talking to. While this may seem manipulative or fictitious to some, I believe that affecting that kind of synchronicity clearly facilitates you to communicate your true emotions more accurately and avoid misinterpretation.

But be cautious. Specialist and author Janine Driver, who spent the last decade teaching federal agents on how to perceive the body language of suspects during investigations, warns that trying to shape your body language can end up backfiring if it is not done skillfully. A possibly risky mistake is to dwell on any information without caring about how it blends into the overall interpretation.

"Attempting to use body language by perusing a dictionary on the body language is like learning to talk French by reading a dictionary in French. Your behaviors appear artificial; your body language abilities seem to be detached from each other." Instead of attempting to modify or disguise your normal body language, I advise you seek to improve and articulate it, such that it enhances rather than distracts you from the meaning you're trying to express.

- Touching the person you speak to (supportive).

- Twirling hair (shortsightedness, insecurity).

- Slump body posture (boredom, isolation).

- Set upright (defensive) body posture.

- Smiling, lean forward (friendly, if not excessive).

- Language of the body, consisting of hand and arm gestures, body stance and motions, and facial gestures and eye movements, can uncover what we think of other people, usually without our realization.

- Cognitive psychologists claim that the human race formed well before spoken human language, the capacity to read implicit physical signals, and to make judgments regarding an individual based on certain signals.

- Like the spoken language, body language appears to change from society to society. Gestures in various countries can have very distinct symbolic meanings.

- By observing non-verbal contact and through teaching yourself, the body language may be intentionally formed to express a desired meaning or perception.

- Manipulation isn't negative.

- To control is to alter the action or mind of someone.

- Manipulation is a conscious force.

You may think about nasty stuff immediately when you listen to the term manipulation. Take a break.

Manipulation isn't negative. People with evil intentions are.

Example 1: Sneaky Deceitful Person

Bad guys are evil. Evil individuals who use manipulation are an issue. For example:

- Cruel girl tries to reduce nice classmate's social status.

- She informs the rest of the class that the person was doing something terrible.

- A nice classmate is less liked.

- The nice classmate feels bad.

Example 2: Cheerful Trickery

Manipulation can turn everyone in a scene look better.

- A party people are experienced tricksters.

- A fun person hits into someone else.

- A party person disarmingly laughs and says sorry, even if the other individual was mistaken.

- Party person doesn't wrestle and has a fantastic evening.

The issue with the instance of mean girl isn't manipulation, her malicious intent, and spreading lies.

My plea: Have positive intentions.

I assume you're going to use the tricks with noble intentions. Please, I request.

Body Language & Mindset

The human brain is judgmental; this is what it is doing. This is what managed to keep us afloat during evolution. In seconds, we pass judgment:

- Is that guy a risk?

- Is the man attractive?

- Is that individual user to my survival (social)?

Beware of this drive, but by no means act upon it without effectively understanding the person. The trickeries below will provoke you to act in a manner that is well viewed.

This segment is not solely regarding body linguistic, but such habits influence the body language on a subconscious level.

Every person deserves to be respected unless otherwise proved.

Again, by treating others with respect, you have everything to acquire and nothing to lose. That doesn't mean you're supposed to caress boots the whole day; it implies you shouldn't ignore or make anyone feel irrelevant.

Just like anyone else, until they do not deserve it.

Outsiders deserve the benefit of the doubt. Anyone can be anything in our universe without having to look like it. I met some kind-looking douche bags and billionaires, who acted like thrilled kids. Look at the book's cover but read a few chapters before you judge.

The douche bag or the billionaire is not 'better' than one another. But being with one made me feel upset, and the other left me feeling good and enthusiastic.

Feel Confident and Express Trust

This is particularly crucial that it requires an essay of its own, and you could never do that all the time. In addition, there are definitely areas where you may not seem convinced to gain likability areas, but the above remains true on average.

With this element, you have two possible approaches. Try doing away with things that make you uneasy. Bad skin to me was a problem that I fixed identical to this. One more was the issue of clothes that I addressed when I took a girl with me while shopping. Work out to help yourself feel safe. I understood plenty from self-help audiobooks. It helped a great deal for me to stay in shape.

All are friends unless otherwise verified. Why burn bridges when you are the one who made them in the first place? No understanding whatsoever:

- Don't have to lose anything.

- You have everything to achieve.

- If this individual would/wants to be a good buddy, you will realize soon enough.

- Always ponder what you can do for someone else.

Do not think when you meet somebody else, "what can they offer me?" But, "what can I offer them, instead?' The best way to support people is to make them want to assist you and everyone wins.

Recognize that I'm not saying that you must give unrequested advice to make yourself look intelligent. Assist people if you genuinely and honestly believe the life of this person would be nicer with the information/help/contact you can give.

Offer assistance but do not insist. Keep it short and let them make their decision.

Entering Inside a Room

The point in time you enter the room is the period you reveal yourself to the people in that room and their judgment. Make sure to take advantage of that.

Some would suggest more severe techniques such as peacocking, but that's not applicable to every situation.

Smile about How Glad You Are to Be Here

Smile whenever you reach a room, no matter where you are. Smile like you really appreciate what you see. Do not overdo it; please do not chuckle loudly. Smile as you walked out and realized the sun was shining.

Accompany the Public

Not to be explicit. Don't yell, "HEY!" Or draw direct attention unless these are individuals who appreciate such conduct. Otherwise, when staring at the individuals in the room, pause a second to stay still or move gradually.

Make Eye Contact

Don't look over the crowd like it's an object. Look at individuals in the eye and smile at them if someone holds your eye contact. Make individuals feel like positive energy has entered the room.

Take Some Time

This demonstrates confidence but also means an open approach.

Wave to Friends (Illusionary)

Humans are hard-wired to love and/or admire people who have friends. Back that up by nodding to your mates and mouthing anything along the lines of "I'll be right there" as you step into space to perform the normal 'greet the crowd' practice.

Here's the thing, to imaginary friends choose to do this. I do this at bigger events all the time. Remember people don't see 360°. If you wave behind them to an inexistent person, they don't know you just waved to empty air.

There are several effects of this:

- People think you know people.

- You have more space to gaze around calmly.

- You'll feel more assured.

The key here is to do so with complete faith, don't smile timidly. Wave like your closest buddy is just across the room and that you are trying to tell them you're going to be there soon.

Posture

The body is always signaling to the people you encounter. Posture impacts snap second judgment people make regarding you but also what you believe about yourself. Additionally, a decent stance is perfect for the back, so what wouldn't you like?

Stand Straight but Easy

Attempt this to find a positive posture:

1. Stand as wide with your feet as your hips

2. Make yourself as tall as doable and assume your head getting pulled up

3. Hold the feeling of being big but relax the shoulders

4. Loosen up your neck and tilt your head, so you don't have to glance up or down with your vision to see a normal human

Few hints:

- Rest when keeping the stance as much as feasible

- Do not puff the chest; it will be straight as though you were lying on the ground

- Steer the shoulders marginally back

Sit up Straight but Not Tight

You can note, as you start sitting up straight, how tiny the majority of people render themselves. When seated at a table, you'll immediately feel very tall. Hold the back straight, but remain as confident as possible.

Have a Certain Tension in the Core

When you're standing or sitting, your abs, back, and overall core should never be deflated/floppy. In general, keep the abs and core under certain stress. Not only does it reinforce well on your pose, but it also makes moving with grace simpler.

Position your feet apart at around the width of the hip.

The feet's stance tells a ton about yourself. It's not an exact science, but normally putting your feet nearer together means insecurity while a larger stance implies confidence.

Both holding the feet excessively close or too far apart can poorly reflect upon you. Seek to find a place where your feet are at hip width or a little further apart, but not much.

Shake Hands

Use a Tender but Firm Handshake

People, in fact, are responsive to how you hold a hand. A handshake with a frail or 'dead fish' would automatically cost you reputation points.

- Don't just 'give' your hand; coordination is what a handshake is.

- Use the force you'd use to pick up a heavy pan stick.

- Don't squeeze too hard if someone offers you a 'dead fish' handshake.

- Allow eye contact while shaking your hand.

- Looking away invariably means something negative.

- You don't care/respect for anyone else.

- There is something you have to hide.

Look at somebody's eyes long enough just to memorize color in their eyes. Just watch for a moment, don't stare.

Smile like They're Making Your Day

While taking a look into someone's eyes during the handshake, smile as if you've seen something that makes you happy in their eyes.

Don't laugh loudly; just smile.

The Face

The face is a very signaling region. There is currently a lot of work on micro-expressions that people subconsciously create. There is a lot of information that people project without realizing it. You will use your face to mark others with details about yourself.

Turn Your Neutral Face Look Happy

Make sure your face appears calm, if not comfortable at rest (e.g., while you are operating on a laptop). It's an easy trick to have a look at your face, as something is slightly fun for you.

Don't Drop Eye Contact Immediately

People are accustomed to pulling away if they meet the eyes of someone. Don't try and do this. Maintain eye contact, and smile. People will often turn down, but there are several individuals who can maintain their attention.

Doing so has several effects:

- People see you as an opener.

- You'll feel more assured.

Please be aware that you must smile when you hold somebody's gaze. It can be quite creepy to look impassively.

How Can I Smile?

Smiling is a really easy trick: pretend you're really seeing something that you really enjoy. Smiling isn't about turning your face in a way; it's about feeling joyful and making your face convey the emotion.

Positioning

The way you position yourself distinguishes how you are viewed. Positioning and posture merged are extremely powerful.

Opening Stance

When you speak to others, place your body so that you're accessible to them. Place yourself ideally in a 'vulnerable' manner. Do not use your arms to protect your chest, do not slouch, etc. This reflects confidence and ease.

Angle Your Body towards the Person You Are Talking to

It is a small change, but it makes a huge difference to make sure your body 'points' to your conversational partner. Placing your body away will imply anxiety, fear, and distrust.

Do Not Lean Yourself on or Against Furniture

Leaning on/against an object (for example, a wall) means passivity and potentially insecure. You should stand with perfect posture as much as you can. Try to develop a pleasant 'neutral stance' using the suggestions from the posture category.

Use Posture When You Have to Lean

If for whatever reason, you have to lean against something, hold on to good posture. Don't slouch.

Behaviors and Techniques

Here I discuss some stuff you should do that mostly require an amount of your conversational/communication data interaction.

Watch Your Posture

Mirroring is a potent method that has been explored a lot. This means that people feel easier around you and that if you stand the way they do, they like you better. For instance:

- They sit with their legs crossed. Cross your legs.

- If they lean on their right leg? You do the same.

- If they are holding a drink? You also grab a drink.

The secret here isn't to be apparent. The instant they actively notice what you are attempting, the method is losing power.

Mirror Moves

You shouldn't be obvious just like with the point above. Yet small things will go a fair way:

- Are you getting a coffee; they grab their cup to take a sip? Do likewise.

- Smile right back as they smile (this is a simple one).

- Are they coming a little closer to you? Do likewise.

Again, don't be blatant, and don't be a weirdo. This method must be used somewhat discreetly, but often.

Chapter 4: 5 NLP Techniques for Beginners

Dissociation

Have you really lived in a position when you were feeling bad? Perhaps you've encountered something that would get you off each time you feel it. Or maybe you're getting nervous in some work environments where you possess to talk out in public. Maybe when you desire to reach that "special person" you've your eye on, you become shy. Although such emotions of sorrow, shyness, or nervousness tend to be inevitable or unavoidable, NLP dissociation strategies may be of tremendous benefit.

1. Classify the emotions (e.g., fear, rage, irritation, a situation dislike) you want to get rid of.

2. Assume you could even glide from your body as well as reflect back on yourself, facing the whole situation from the perspective of an observer.

3. Notice the sensation is changing dramatically.

4. Assume you will fly from your body gazing at yourself for an additional lift, so fly out of your form again, and you smile at yourself and feel for yourself. The dual disconnection should deprive almost any slight situation of the negative feeling.

Everyone experiences a bad day when a situation ruins it and gives one a bad feeling. This may be an experience that drowns your spirit every time you face it. Also, it may be a certain nervous feeling that comes at any point that you have to address an audience. It could be a feeling of shyness that comes whenever you need to approach a certain (special) person.

Although it may seem as though this feeling of shyness, sadness or nervousness is automatic and unstoppable, what the NLP technique of dissociation offers are ways to get over these feelings.

Get to know about the emotion that you wish to overcome whether it is a feeling of discomfort, anger, or dislike for a certain situation.

Imagine the possibility of teleportation and looking back at yourself going through the same situation, but this time from an observer's point of view.

Take note of the dramatic change that occurs in the feelings.

To get an extra boost for your morale, think about floating out of your body and watching yourself. This means that you will now be looking at yourself while your other self is also looking at yourself. What this double dissociation attempts to do is to take away all the negative emotions in all possible minor situations.

Do you ever wish that you could somehow step back from your most distressing or destructive thoughts or somehow take a break from your own mind? This dissociation exercise can help you do just that. It provides you with a quick sense of emotional relief, allowing you to take on the role of an objective observer. This helps you not only react in a more constructive way to emotive situations, but also helps you in keeping your temper when others annoy you. Therefore, this exercise can be helpful in improving your relationships. It is especially good for recurring fears and phobias.

To see how this technique works, let's imagine that your working life is more difficult than it ought to be because you become nervous whenever you see your boss, who is frequently in the office. Because he makes you nervous, your productivity is impaired, and so you decide to use this technique to lessen these negative feelings.

Firstly, conjure up a mental image or 'mental movie' of the scene. The important aspect of this step is to imagine yourself not from your own perspective, but as an impartial third party who has just happened to come into the room and watch the scenario unfold. To continue with the example stated above, you would imagine watching yourself working at your desk, seeing your boss come in through the door and starting to show signs of anxiety such as foot-tapping, sweating, and shuffling papers around. You would imagine watching yourself greet your boss in an anxious tone of voice.

Once you have imagined the scene as an objective observer, it's now time to manipulate the movie! Firstly, play it backwards. That's right—do a mental re-wind. If you have ever rewound a DVD or video, you will know that this typically looks quite comical, and so when you apply a similar effect to your mental movie, your emotional response should start to dampen immediately. Do this a couple of times—watch the 'movie' in your mind's eye, then rewind.

The next step is to add some light-hearted music to the film mentally. Watch the film being rewound as the amusing music plays. Do these two or three times. By this point, the emotional response previously triggered by the memory or fear should have changed significantly. If not, simply repeat the above steps a few more times until you have well and truly loosened your old associations between that particular mental image and certain unwanted feelings.

Reframing Content

This technique is useful for all the times you feel like you are trapped in a negative or helpless situation. With the help of reframing, you will be able to get rid of all negative situations by becoming empowered by interpreting the meaning of the situation into becoming a positive thing.

Take a situation where your relationship ended, for instance. Although it may seem as if it is, an awful situation when one looks at it on the surface, what about the possibility of those hidden benefits of being single? Think of the fact that you are now open to meeting and interacting with new people, which means that it is possible for you to get into a new relationship. This means that you are now free to do whatever you want to do at whatever time you want to do it. From the last relationship that ended, you must have learned some valuable lessons that will eventually be useful to you in your subsequent relationship(s).

It is very possible to panic or be thrown into fear in certain situations. Instead of focusing on fear, you can sway your focus by reframing. This will contribute to helping you make some even-handed and responsible decisions.

Attempt this method if you feel down or helpless in a scenario. Reframing can take every unpleasant scenario to inspire you by having you constructive regarding the sense of the event.

Let's presume you end your love, for starters. At the top, that can sound horrible, so let's reframe it. What seems to be the advantages of becoming single? You're now accessible to certain future partnerships, for starters. You have the right to do anything you want, anytime you want to. And from this relationship, you have gained important lessons that will enable you to have much better future relationships.

All these are instances of having a situation reframed. You offer yourself a new understanding of this by reframing the context of the breakup.

It's normal to worry or dwell on anxiety in planned circumstances, but that just contributes to even more issues. In comparison, turning your attention to the way you have just mentioned helps clear your mind and make rational, even-handed choices.

This technique will help you change your feelings towards a particular event. This will further your ability to handle even difficult situations, and in turn, will boost your confidence. Your intention here isn't to adopt an unconditionally positive view of a situation — that would be an unrealistic goal, and in any event, it isn't practical to deliberately overlook negative aspects of our lives just because we wish things were different! However, we can choose to take a more positive attitude to almost any event without losing our grip on reality. Reframing helps you do just that. This lessens the hold that particular memories have over you and leaves you free to pursue a more positive future.

To begin with, pick a memory or problem that persistently leaves you feeling unhappy whenever you think of it. For instance, let's imagine you have recently lost your job and are in the process of looking for new employment. Looking for a job can be hard work, and some days you might find yourself dwelling on the fact that you were fired, that you feel bad, and that life is tough. This kind of thought will not inspire you to move forward. You need to find a way of reconceptualizing it so as to minimize its psychological impact.

To reframe a memory, start by calling it to mind:

- Mentally imagine the scene.

- Blow it up bigger and bigger, until you 'feel' as though you were there all over again.

- Notice how you feel. In the example mentioned above, you might feel angry and powerless.

Now consciously reframe the situation. Imagine taking a couple of steps back from the mental image. Shrink it a little in your mind's eye.

Consider how you could view the situation in a positive way. For instance, leaving your job allows you the opportunity to find a new position and shake up your life for the better. Really, make an effort to think about the same situation but from a new angle. Encourage this new emotion—hope, excitement, or even relief if you hated your old job—to overwhelm you. Focus on these feelings as you look again at the memory in your mind's eye. Repeat this exercise until your primary response to the memory in question is positive rather than negative.

Anchoring Yourself

Centering originates from the Russian psychologist Ivan Pavlov that performed with dogs by constantly circling a bell as the dogs feed. After frequent bell rings, he found that by ringing a bell at any time, he can get the pets to drool, even if there's no meat available.

It produced a neural connection between both the bell as well as salivating actions called a programmed response.

You should use all kinds of "anchors" stimulus-response yourself!

Anchoring yourself lets you connect your desired optimistic emotional reaction to a particular expression or feeling. When selecting a happy emotion or image, then consciously attaching it to a specific action, you will activate this anchor anytime you feel weak, then your emotions will shift automatically.

1. Recognize what you expect to experience (for starters, confidence, joy, peacefulness, etc.).

2. Decide where you like this anchor to be on your body, like grabbing the earlobe, rubbing your thumb, or gripping a

fingertip. This body interaction would cause the good feeling to be stimulated at will. Wherever you pick, it doesn't matter as much as it's a special experience you're not touching for anything specific.

3. Think of a moment in the background where you have known the condition (e.g., confidence). Go back to the period mentally and float through your body, gaze into your eyes & relive the moment. Adapt your physical language to suit state and memory. Look at what you've done, know what you've heard & feel when you recall your memory. You are going to start experiencing the condition. That is equivalent to reading a buddy an amusing tale from memory, so when you "join" the narrative, you start smiling again, as you are "associating" with the tale so "reliving" it.

4. As you return to memory, pull/touch/shove the area you've chosen on the body. When you reenact the memory, you'll see the sensation swell. The instant the relational condition rises, remove the pressure, and continue wearing off.

5. This will establish stimulus-response neurology that will activate the condition if you render the contact again. Only contact yourself again in the same manner to experience the condition (e.g., esteem).

6. Think of another experience where you feel the condition, look through and revisit it with your eyes, and hold the condition in the same place as before, to make the reaction even better. The anchor gets more effective each time you bring another

recollection and will activate a greater reaction.

7. Using this strategy, anytime you want, your attitude is modified.

This process of creating a neurological connection between the ringing of a bell and the attitude of salivating is known as a conditioned response. These responses to stimulus anchors can also be used on humans.

The result of anchoring oneself is that a person gets to link a desired positive emotional response with a specific sensation or a phrase. When you can select a positive emotion or a thought and intentionally link it to a gesture, you will be able to trigger the anchor at every point you feel low, so you will be able to change your feelings immediately. Here are some ways of anchoring yourself:

Take note of the feelings you want to experience. It could be a feeling of happiness, confidence, calmness, *etc.* Decide on the part of your body where you would love to place the anchor. This could be a certain action like pulling your earlobe, squeezing your fingernail, or touching your knuckle. With this physical touch, you will be able to trigger the desired positive feeling whenever you want to. This has nothing to do with the part of the body that you have chosen; all that needs to be done is create that connection between the unique touch and the feelings. You do not have to make this touch for anything else besides the feeling.

Think about a certain time in the past when you had the same feelings you are experiencing at a given moment. Reminisce on the time you felt the same way, then float into your body by looking through your eyes so that you will be able to replay and relive the memory.

Once this is done, you can make some adjustments to your body language to match with the memory and the state of mind. When you are reliving the memory, make sure you can see, hear, and feel everything the way you remember it. If you can do this, the feeling will come back, just as it will when you tell a funny story from the past to your friend.

Keep in mind that you will typically begin to laugh over again as you tell the story because while you get into the story, you will create some mental association with the story and relive the experience.

While you are going back to this memory, pull, touch, or squeeze that part of your body that you had earlier chosen. If you do this, you will notice that the feeling will heighten while you are reliving the memory. Once the emotional state gets to its peak and begins to wear off, you can then release the touch.

This touch will create a certain neurological response that will trigger the state whenever you touch that spot again. So, in order to feel this state again, all you need to do is touch yourself again in the same way.

To get an even stronger response, you can think of another memory from the past where you had that same feeling and go back and relive it from your own perspective. Anchor that same state as you have done before. Every time you add another memory, this anchor will gain more potency so that it will trigger an even stronger response.

Whenever you feel the need to change your mood, you can revisit this technique.

There are different moments when NLP anchoring can be used; the most common is in rewarding someone. Take the case of a grade two mathematics teacher who pats his or her students on their backs whenever they pass, and for those who don't pass, they don't get a pat as a reward. The students will strive to pass their exams so that they get a reward. By using the pat on their back, the students have attributed the pat on the back with doing well or the sense of having it under control, therefore before a test, the teacher can use this pat on the back to remind them that they have everything under control and they would do well, effectively calming nerves and jitters before a test.

Similarly, a martial arts coach can use anchoring to improve his student's feeling of reward whenever they do well, for instance, after sparring. Traditionally after a spar, the fighters will shake their hands; a coach who feels his student has put up a good fight can give a light punch on their arm to show this. Sparring is an intense session that is accompanied by adrenaline and endorphins (pleasurable feeling) when the coach uses the light punch on the arm as an anchor after the handshake. The students will associate the post adrenaline endorphins with the reward. Later on, before a fight or before grading by judges, the coach can use this anchor (the light punch) to help their students calm their nerves by giving them a light punch on the shoulder.

Neuro-linguistic Programming anchoring can also be employed in seduction as will be explained in detail later on in this book. In the meantime, though try doing an exercise of applying to anchor on either yourself or someone you work with, spouse or kids. It may take a while before you see the results; therefore good luck and remember that practice makes perfect.

Swish

The swish pattern is a Neuro-linguistic Programming technique that is used in replacing an unfavorable behavior or emotion with a more useful one. It is a copy and paste system where you copy the emotion associated with doing one thing and pasting over the emotion elicited by another. It can be used to make the "bad" activities such as going to the gym and eating salad seem better by applying a different emotion such as the happy emotion elicited when eating a chocolate cake. The idea of the swish technique is to keep on switching back and forth between two images with one feeling in mind.

Imagine you have changed your jobs and tomorrow you start work at a new company, the idea of going to a new environment is scary, you will feel anxious about meeting a new boss, how will you fit in with your colleagues, will they like you, will you like them. Is it the wrong decision for you to change jobs? These questions will elicit feelings of worry, anxiety, and nervousness, among others. The odds of you projecting these feelings to the new employees are very high if this is what you will be feeling; therefore, you must swap the feeling of anxiety whenever you think of the first day at work with a more comfortable feeling like excitement. How do you do this?

First, think of a memory that got you excited, like going to the fun park when you were younger, or attending a party with your friends; think about the emotion, the excitement of adventure you will have while thinking about this quickly switch to the thought of your first day at work tomorrow and right before the feeling of anxiety creeps in a switch back to the idea of going out with friends. Do this a couple of times, holding onto the feeling of excitement as you "swish" back and forth between the two mental pictures. As this is happening, the conscious memory is trying to blind the subconscious memory into associating the good feeling with both events to overcome the bad memory.

Very few of us like exercising, no one like the pain and the aches that come with hitting the gym every single time. The idea of the soreness and how tired we will be after the exercises; it is no wonder people have gym memberships that they rarely utilize fully. How about a little exercise, before you groan, I mean a mental exercise, think about going to a camp with your family or friends. The adventure, the thrill of sleeping out by the fire, the joy of exchanging stories around the bonfire, the amazing nights of roasting meat, and marshmallows under the stars. Now think about going to the gym, think about the different people you will meet there, think about the campfire and the different people who you just met seated around the campfire, think about the gym and the different equipment there, think about the camp and the different equipment and supplies you will need for camping; do this several times switch back and forth between the two mental pictures without letting the positive feeling disappear. After about ten times of this swishing, you will be feeling pretty excited about going to the gym and ready for the adventure. If it doesn't work, do it again with a different thought that you are particularly excited. Remember, you need to do a lot of practice to master this technique.

Grounding

This is an excellent basic exercise that sets the stage for many other NLP practices. In grounding yourself, you are immediately exerting a calming effect on your body and mind. This will make you more receptive to NLP exercises, increasing the chances of rapid and lasting change. It can also be used as a simple, effective means of inducing a relaxed state whenever and wherever you like. If you are having a stressful morning at work, for example, shut the office door for a few minutes and get ready to feel better quickly.

Begin by removing your shoes and socks. Stand with your feet flat on the ground. If possible, do this exercise outdoors to make it extra relaxing! Take deep breaths in and out. Stand with your arms held loosely by your sides, with your feet approximately shoulder-width apart. Close your eyes. Now imagine yourself anchored to the ground in such a way that nothing can unbalance or disturb you.

Wriggle your toes slightly and imagine that they are holding onto the ground beneath you, holding you steady. Keep your legs straight but avoid locking your knees. Inhale, then as you release the breath, make a conscious effort to drop your shoulders slightly. Imagine, as you exhale, your feelings of tension and worry leaving your body.

Once you are in a relaxed state, shift your attention to your lower abdomen, 2–3 inches below your belly button. Make yourself aware of the tension in those muscles and how they hold you upright. Realize how grounded you now feel. Open your eyes and keep your gaze soft and steady. Tell yourself how relaxed you are and how you can cope with anything life throws at you. Keep your breathing deep and even.

Practice this exercise for a few minutes every day, and you will begin to feel naturally more grounded without trying. Be sure to re-direct your attention to that point below your navel every so often. This way, you are teaching yourself to feel calm, relaxed, and unruffled whenever you shift your focus to that part of your body.

After a few days, try maintaining this state of relaxation and grounded-ness as you walk around. With practice, you will be able to induce a highly relaxed, confident state whenever you need it. This technique is invaluable in high-pressure situations such as job interviews or having a high-stakes conversation with someone you respect and admire.

Chapter 5: 4 Advanced Techniques for Your NLP Learning

Confidence Visualization

What separates confident people from those with low self-esteem and relatively lower levels of belief in their own capabilities? One important factor is their ability to imagine more favorable outcomes. Remember, a key assumption in NLP is that the mind exerts a powerful effect on the body, and vice versa. When you envisage a certain mental or physical state for yourself, the more likely it is that you will be able to access and sustain it.

Close your eyes and imagine that you have suddenly been cloned. Take a minute to imagine this carbon copy of you, so that its existence feels as real as you can possibly make it. Now picture your identical twin standing or sitting opposite you. Begin by imagining them to be exactly the same as you.

The next step is to mold them gradually into a confident individual who knows that they can achieve whatever they want to get from life. For example, you could imagine your clone to have better posture, a louder and smoother speaking voice, and a confident smile. Take your time to imagine these details. Make the transformation as vivid as possible. Notice how this cloned and altered version of you moves and talks. What is their energy or 'vibe' like? How would other people know that they are a confident person?

Once you have built a steady image of this new version of yourself, imagine stepping forward and into the body of this clone. You should automatically feel yourself beginning to adopt the posture and way of speaking. Smile and take a deep breath in, imagining as you do so that you are absorbing all the very best qualities of this other 'you'.

Whiteout

If you find yourself thinking the same old troublesome memories time and time again or suffer from intrusive thinking, using a whiteout technique can bring you great relief. Whiting out a mental image lessens the emotional effect it has on you, and with regular practice, you will soon find that it will lose its power to impact you at all.

Close your eyes and bring to mind a mental image that causes you trouble. It may be an embarrassing memory or a painful scene from your past. It could even be something that hasn't actually happened, but still represents a source of torment — you may be plagued by a particular fear around public speaking, perhaps imagining yourself forgetting your words or blushing uncontrollably. Whatever the image, bring it to mind and concentrate on it.

The next step should be done rapidly and decisively. Imagine seeing the image in full color, but then turning up the brightness so much that it is literally whited out. If you have ever experimented with the brightness settings on a digital camera or image manipulation software, you could use this as a 'model' for what such a whiteout would look like.

Take a deep breath and distract yourself by thinking of something neutral and totally unrelated to the mental image with which you are working. Then repeat the steps outlined above, taking a few moments between each 'round' of whiting out to think of another topic. This gives your brain a chance to solidify the connection between the mental image and the act of whiting it out.

Do this enough times and after a while, you will struggle to remember the original image at all. Even if you do, the effect it has on you will likely be greatly diminished. You can do this for as many memories or other kinds of images as you like.

Creating Rapport

NLP isn't just applicable to the messages you send to yourself. It's also about creating and sustaining better-quality relationships with other people. If you stop and think about it, human relationships make the world go around. Whether it's smoothing over interactions with your family, increasing the strength of your friendships or closing an important business deal, it's useful to have the skills required to 'tap into' other peoples' thoughts and feelings.

A good way to appear more approachable, friendly and empathic is to learn to build rapport with other people. NLP practitioners use a few techniques to facilitate this. Firstly, they stress the importance of body language. Have you ever noticed that the way you hold yourself has a huge impact on the way you feel? It's difficult to sustain a happy, upbeat mood if you sit with your shoulders slumped, for example. Now think about how other peoples' body language makes you feel. If you've ever arrived at home or at the office feeling upbeat and glad to be alive only to be

134

confronted by a sullen relative or co-worker who clearly communicating dissatisfaction via their body language, you will be all too familiar with the power that other peoples' posture and facial expression can have!

Fortunately, you can also use this piece of psychology for the power of good. When you next want to develop a sense of closeness and understanding with someone else, subtly match their body language. Humans naturally feel more comfortable with those who appear to understand us and share our thoughts and opinions. We may not consciously realize it, but when someone else's body language mirrors our own, we feel reassured.

However, you need to be careful when mirroring so as not to appear too obvious! Do not immediately copy every single thing your conversation partner is doing. Rather, mimic only a few gestures, and allow a few seconds to elapse before shifting your own limbs or changing your facial expression.

A more advanced technique is known as 'pacing.' To pace someone is to make them follow your lead without them even realizing what you are trying to do. An experienced NLP practitioner is able to use his or her body language skills to build rapport and then influence the other party into thinking, feeling, or behaving a certain way.

For example, let's say that your colleague is having a bad day at work, and their negativity is draining you. You want them to feel more excited about the project your team is working on and lift their mood. To pace them, you could start by holding a conversation in which you match their body language—you may speak quietly, move slowly, and adopt a slightly slumped posture to echo what they are currently feeling. However, after a few minutes, you could begin to adopt more positive movements and change your voice to a more energetic, upbeat tone. You would pay attention to the way in which your co-worker responds to you. If you are skilled at pacing, you would notice that they would gradually start to mirror your positive body language, and because the mind follows where the body leads, they would begin to feel more cheerful. By the end of the conversation – and the entire interaction need last no longer than 20–30 minutes to elicit such a result – you would both be feeling good!

Finally, another useful NLP technique in building rapport is to share in your partner's submodalities. A submodality is simply a way of communicating and interpreting information via the senses – we can communicate via touch, taste, hearing, and so on. If you can tune in to the submodality favoured by another person, you can adjust your own communication accordingly.

They will then feel as though you understand them more readily.

The best way to access someone's preferred submodality is to listen carefully to their choice of words. For instance, suppose you are talking to a client in an attempt to negotiate a deal and you want to build a rapport with them. Listening to them speak, you may pick up phrases that indicate they are in a visual or 'seeing' submodality – 'I can picture it', they might say, or 'I'm seeing a particular vision of...,' and so on. This is a valuable information because it allows you to mirror their preferred verbal communication in much the same way as their body language. You can then weave visual-based words and phrases into the conversation, perhaps saying things like 'If we consider the bigger picture...' or 'Our company has the foresight to meet your future needs'. This is a subtle but effective way of building rapport. The other party will feel as

138

though you are on their wavelength and will be more likely to trust and respect you as a result.

Future Pacing

This is another technique that you can work with, in which you will ask a person to imagine that they are doing something in the future, and then you will monitor the reaction that they have to this. It is typically something that is going to be used in order to check that a change process has been successful. You can check this out by observing the body language of the target when this person is going through a difficult situation before and after the intervention.

The theory of this is that, once the person has taken the time to visualize the experience in a positive way, when they do actually encounter the situation, the visualized situation that they did before is going to be their model for how to behave in that situation, even those they only imagined and made up the visualization. The mind is not really able to come up with the differences between the real-life scenario and the imagined one, which can help the person to get through that whole situation much easier.

So, how is this going to be useful for the person who is trying to work with dark NLP? If you are worried about a specific situation, then the idea of future pacing is going to be able to help you out here. Before entering into that situation, take some time to visualize it in your head. Think about it in a positive way, imagining what it will feel like if that situation goes really well, above your own expectations, and if you were able to get through it without a hitch.

Try to imagine this as clearly as possible. Let's say that you are anxious about a job interview. Imagine what you are going to wear to the interview, what time you will show up, what you will say about your resume, and the answers you are going to give to the questions you are asked. Imagine that you are shaking the hand of the person interviewing you and that you feel really good about the whole situation like you are sure that they will offer you the job because they were dazzled by your credentials and all of the things you said during the interview.

You will find that if you were able to come up with a strong enough and clear enough picture and visualization of the event, that when you actually head to the real event, it won't seem so scary. Your brain will assume that it has already gone through all of this, and the situation is going to pan out much better than you would imagine.

Chapter 6: The secret method: Reach your subconscious mind and overcome anxiety

Re-programming your subconscious

Below, right now, deny residing in your own negative thoughts more. All its functions would be to create your energy down a level and encircle you with a feeling that prevents such a thing besides coming back to your own life.

1. Whenever a negative idea concerning the last pops up emotionally yell the term "stop!" or envision a person blowing a whistle anything that may disrupt those well-worn nerve pathway grooves. Sometimes I will sing a song just as

loudly as I could either aloud or within my own mind. Your goal here will be to consciously take charge of one's own subconscious.

2. When you've disrupted this. Thought pattern, replace it with a favorable memory that is equally powerful. For example, say you're mistreated as a youngster and a certain event pops to mind. Rather than giving into the memory, then bring a joyful memory you've got and remember it at as much detail as feasible.

3. In case you have hardly any joyful memories, or even believe it is tough to think of something when anger or annoyance attack, produce a set of some joyous occasions if you are in a fantastic mood and browse this list whenever you are feeling down.

4. You could even write down prospective events you would like to see. In the event that you were really poor connection, then write what you need on another relationship (be honest though

nobody's perfect!). Jot down exactly what your own perspective partner would soon be enjoying plus some joyful times you may love to share with you along with him/her. Additionally, this is an excellent solution to program your own mind and energy field to bring everything you desire.

The last is gone, it is performed and over. The only way that you may have some effect you currently will be if you allow it to. People's "bad memory" paths have worn a groove on the mind; therefore, it is a whole lot easier to remember them whether people want it or maybe not. Elect to reprogram your mind and realize the big difference it makes on your mood, and also on your own life.

It's remarkably natural to demand yourself with the unwanted things constantly that can be called negative self-talk. In the event that you may use the energy of positive affirmation and equipped to replicate it in yourself, this ability will allow one to restrain the human mind. This attitude may change your believing structure at any circumstance and also the method of your own feelings.

Getting optimistic is unexpectedly beneficial. This item can help become stronger and boost your self-esteem. This attitude will permit you to go away from the adverse believing. Anybody who wished to improve life instantly should make use of the energy. Anybody can replace her or his unwelcome beliefs into powerful beliefs by injuries thought procedure. It's obtainable.

Powerful Tool to Get Rid of Anxiety

Anxiety is the body's automatic and innate response that occurs due to the stress that you go through. It also can be described as the sensation of fear and worry about something in the future. Anxiety is of different types which are classified according to the degree to which anxiety takes place. One of the most powerful tools that are used to guide individuals with anxiety is NLP.

Keep "you" on top of the priority list

Give yourself enough time. One of the most negative things that we do is forgetting to treat ourselves; this can be unhealthy. To treat yourself, you need to begin your day by doing something that you like, such as dancing, jogging, listening to music, *etc.* By doing this, you can non-verbally shout out to the world that you are always the first on your list.

Keep in mind the feeling that triggers your anxiety

Fantasize the event or the person that causes the feeling of anxiety in you, pay attention to it closely as you can. Notice where the pain in your body is when you start feeling anxious. Is it in your stomach? Your chest? Your hands? Where is it? Pay attention to how these feelings are unstable; they don't stay still. They keep moving from one

147

place to the other. Notice this unstable pain and try to make it move faster. At the initial stage, you are going to feel pain and suffering, but that is a good sign; it signifies that you control yourself and that an outside event is not controlling you.

Give this unstable ball of pain a color

Give this mobile ball a red color and now take notice of the direction that the ball is moving. Now try to take this object outside your body and pay attention to it. Make the ball into a blue color through your imagination and change its direction of moving. Visualize this blue ball moving in the opposite direction into your body. Now take notice of the movement of the ball, you will notice that this movement gives you a different feeling, a feeling that is way much better than the feeling that you went through before. Imagine something that makes you feel good and gives your comfort; pay attention to how it makes you feel, and then mix this feeling of comfort with the blue object that is spinning in you. Pay attention to everything that is around you, including your breathing. Now relax and calm yourself.

Think of good things before bed

Don't allow yourself to think of things that have negatively impacted you or seem problematic to you. Thinking of something that negatively affects you before going to bed makes you more stressed, worried, and anxious. Try to end your day by thinking and feeling things that cause positive responses in your body.

By training your mind to increase positivity and boost your confidence, you will be able to increase the level of esteem you have about yourself. You will be an individual who perceives yourself and others more optimistically. By following these techniques, you will be able to develop into an individual with empathy. You will be able to face real-life situations with strength, power, and confidence, which will help you to lead a more productive and successful life.

NLP for Fears and Phobias

Fears and phobias are serious issues for many of us. We might have a slight fear of getting into a car accident (realistic) or a phobia that spiders will bite us at random (unrealistic). Fortunately, NLP has served as a serious help for those trying to cope with fears.

Swishing

While we talked about the swish technique earlier, you may not have realized how effective it could be in overcoming certain fears. Most specifically, it is helpful in getting over the fear of public speaking. If you are nervous about a presentation, you want to change that emotion to one of excitement. Easier said than done – until now.

Using this example of public speaking anxiety, we can demonstrate how you might use swishing to create a better reality. For starters, you need to find a memory where you remember being truly excited. You were anticipating something big – and it felt good. Take turns thinking of that memory and then anticipating tomorrow's big presentation. The key is to swap the thoughts so fast that you do not even have time to think about how nervous you are. You will soon associate the presentation with excitement.

Coping with PTSD

For some of us, post-traumatic stress disorder (PTSD) is a reality. In order to treat PTSD, NLP practitioners may suggest a process that involves visualization and exposure. Treatment typically starts with brief exposure to the trigger in a non-threatening environment. For instance, the spider might be in a jar or a film with a trigger might be played. Next, the patient will visualize a past incident as if he or she is watching it on film. It may be less threatening to see it in black and white and then eventually move into color. Exposure might be presented again in another safe place. The practitioner will address any difference in your response.

Coping with Phobias

If you are having problems with other types of fears, you can use the same technique described above for PTSD. Instead of using a past event, you will think about the stimulus you are afraid of.

Some fears are healthy and "normal" for us to have. For example, it is healthy to have a fear of falling from a very tall platform. On the other hand, a fear of climbing a step ladder is not very healthy at all.

Envision your fear on a big screen but try to obscure it so that it is less threatening. You can do this by making the screen smaller, making the video fuzzy or even changing its colors.

As you watch this video in your head, imagine a time where you had a lot of confidence and happiness. Think about a time you were strong. Swish this memory with the video you are watching in your head until you feel just fine with the trigger stimulus.

How to rewire your brain to be less anxious

Managing stress and anxiety may be finished with the ideal advice accessible. Stress and stress affect individuals in many walks of life. You are one of many who believe isolated. Have a look at forums and community classes where you will discover countless people that are afflicted as you're. It will not also need to be considered a losing struggle and you can find means so as to handle this painful issue. Medications and drugs are readily available to help combat it we must prefer the non-toxic and natural remedies in managing tension and stress.

Decide on a period where you can fulfill your day with your pals. Talking and sharing about your issues using them may diminish your stress levels immediately. Requesting sound advice can offer you various options about what best to manage stressful conditions.

Schedule off time out of the hectic day and focus on pampering yourself. Treat yourself into a nice hot bubble bath, go running, buy or simply relax with a fantastic novel. Tasks such as these may simply take away your mind from everyday pressures and anxieties.

Stress and anxiety are generally brought around by life's failures and disappointments. Our aims in life help us focus and establishing attainable goals will encourage us to get what you would like to realize. Setting small goals brings us nearer to that particular one huge goal, one step at the same time. It is going to surely offer an enormous ego boost and function as a trust builder every single time we reach our objectives. We'll soon be equipped in managing stress and anxiety.

You may want to try out writing in a journal. Many men and women find it therapeutic to write their thoughts down and feelings. You can be more aware of the things which cause one to be stressed and stressed. You can avoid those scenarios as you have identified them, or you might be prepared to take care of the situation since they happen appropriately.

What is it about anxiety that is terrible to the point that generally advanced individuals are rushed to escape it? The impressions of fate or fear or panic felt by sufferers are genuinely overpowering - the extremely same sensations, actually, that an individual would feel if the most noticeably terrible truly were going on. Over and over again, these, actually, fearful, sickening sensations drive customers to the moment the help of the drug, which is promptly accessible and considered by numerous insurance agencies to be mainline of treatment. Also, what great specialist would propose skirting the prescriptions when an enduring patient can get symptomatic help rapidly?

Tips for Overcoming Fears

Each of us has a fear that we would like to overcome. If you are struggling with fears of your own, these tips might help with a bit of assistance from neuro-linguistic programming. Try them out for yourself to see how effective they can be:

Start with the smallest fears and then branch outward. Not only will this help you build a strong sense of positivity and self-esteem, but it will also motivate you to move forward.

- Take your fear outside of your comfort zone. Go to the zoo to combat your fear of

156

reptiles, rather than bringing them into your home. This will also help you create an anchor that will work in your favor.

- Use future pacing to think about how you will act when confronted with a similar issue in the future. For instance, you might have a different reaction to the stimulus the next time you encounter it now that you have worked to create anchors and visualize it. Discuss specific steps you can take to make the situation as calming and relaxing as possible.

- Maintain a positive attitude whenever it is possible to do so. You might be surprised at how well you are able to overcome fears when you are looking at the bright side of life. Not everything has to be incredibly negative!

- Finding new ways to dissociate from your fears (and other harmful emotions) is a great choice. It keeps you from identifying too closely with an emotion that you are trying to avoid. It might also help if you are laughing and smiling while you envision the video. You will feel much better the next time you come into contact with the physical stimulus.

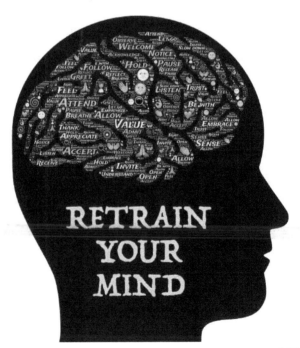

Chapter 7: Flexibility and Adaptability

There are four main points to NLP. They are referred to as the Pillars of NLP. They are behavioral flexibility, rapport, outcome thinking, and sensory awareness. Each one is of equal importance as the others. Taking the time to look briefly at each one of these points gives a better understanding of NLP as a whole and how it can help you weed out the fakers in your life.

The first pillar is Behavioral Flexibility. Basically, this means going with the flow. When people can see that, the tactic they are currently using isn't working and adapt their behavior it can have great results. Being able to change your perspective quickly will allow more people to understand you.

The next aspect we are going to look at is rapport. Creating a good rapport with someone is simply getting him or her to trust you quickly. In addition, it is the ability to form quick relationships with people. It is easy to build rapport by using common language, being polite, and showing empathy. There are many ways to build a good rapport with a person; these are only a few.

Then we move on to outcome thinking. It is exactly what it states, spending the time to think about the end result of what you want. Oftentimes, people are stuck on a certain point that is commonly negative. It consumes the thought pattern and can make choosing the correct route to where you actually want to go difficult. With outcome thinking, you are always working toward an end goal. This can promote better decision making along the way.

Lastly, we have sensory awareness. Being aware of the surroundings contributes to knowing what is actually going on. When you walk into a public place and you take notice of the tone of the room, the colors surrounding you, the groups of people, it can be very enlightening. It can also help you easily understand how you need to behave in that situation.

The more you learn about these four pillars, the more success you will have with NLP. They are the foundation and anyone who wants to learn NLP will spend a lot of time on each one. Gaining more knowledgeable helps you apply what you have learned to your daily life and the more protected you will be from the ones that want to manipulate you, control you, or cause other burdens in your life.

NLP has grown and changed over the years. What started out as focusing on what people's eyes were doing, the words they choose to use, and building quick rapport, turned into something more. All sciences grow and change over the course of time and we imagine that this one will also continue to evolve.

After focusing on what the eyes were doing, word choice, and rapport, this therapy started to grow and focus on other aspects. In the 80's, the people using NLP were focusing on what it is that causes feelings inside of us. This helped therapists to figure out how to help someone deal with their individual problems.

More and more people started using the techniques found with NLP, but they wanted to put different names to it. To say they had come up with it all on their own. When it comes down to it, no matter what you call it, NLP is the same across the globe. Today, it is used not only to help you have control and choices in how you react, but it can also help you figure out what other people are up to.

The people here and now who are using NLP have a variety of different reasons for doing it. Some of it is to help them become better people, while for others; it is about weeding out the rats in their lives. Businesses use it in team-building and marketing techniques. Here again, we can see how vast the world of Neuro-Linguistic Programming really is.

It has been said that people who study Neuro-Linguistic Programming live freely. They have the ability to access all different types of situations and make choices in how they choose to proceed instead of being led by instinct and emotion. How you think, feel, behave, and speak can all be choices you make that can help you lead the best life possible.

What Works with Neuro-Linguistic Programming?

Core aspects of neuro-linguistic learning include planning, intervention, and efficient communication. The idea is that if an entity can comprehend how another individual executes a function, then the machine can be replicated and transmitted to others so that they can execute the job, too.

Neuro-linguistic programming advocates suggest that everybody would have a personal map of the truth. To build a comprehensive summary of one case, those that conduct NLP examine their own from other viewpoints. The NLP patient receives insight from an awareness of a variety of viewpoints. Advocates in this line of thinking claim that the perceptions are essential to the perception of the knowledge accessible, and also that the mind and body control one another. Neuro-linguistic programming seems to be a methodology that is experiential. Therefore, in order to benefit from the practice, if an individual wish to comprehend an action, they must conduct the same action.

NLP professionals claim thinking, collaboration, and transformation are inherent hierarchies. The six conceptual improvements are:

Intent & Spirituality

These can include something greater than one's own, such as faith, philosophy, or any framework. That is the most elevated degree of transition.

Identification

Identification is the individual you claim to be, which involves the responsibilities as well as the positions you perform in life.

Convictions and Values

They are the set of moral convictions, as well as the questions that matter for you.

Talents and Competencies

What are the talents? And what you should achieve?

Habits

The basic acts you do are habits.

Environment

The background or atmosphere of the context, or the other individuals around you. This really is the least exchange rate.

Increasing the conceptual level has the function of organizing and coordinating the details beneath. As a consequence, having a lower-level adjustment will trigger higher-level adjustments. Due to the NLP hypothesis, having a difference in such a higher stage would often result in improvements in the lowest stages.

Rapport

Ultimately, NLP is built upon rapport—the ability to relate to each other. To have a rapport with someone else is to have a connection with them—it is a sort of camaraderie that you see between friends that makes our minds even more connected than we are probably aware of. Have you ever been to a restaurant and decide to watch people? If you've never done it before, try it—look for a couple that looks like they've been together for a long while. What do you notice about how they move?

Most of the time, as our relationships build, we create rapport with each other. We create this ability to understand each other at a deeper level, and this is usually shown by taking a look at how we move around each other. People who have a solid rapport with each other usually tend to move at the same time. They mirror each other — this process shows that they are connected closely. You will usually breathe, walk, eat, and drink at the same pace as your friend if you are together. You will naturally synchronize your steps together. You will stand in the same poses. You will probably also do other things together at the same time. This is because, when you like someone else, your mind sort of synchronizes with them. It is a part of our non-verbal communication. We see our friend doing something, and unconsciously, we shift to do the same thing. This is natural; we do it because we want to make sure that we are constantly in the same positions as those around us. We crave to be liked, we crave to be connected to people, and ultimately, the way that we achieve that likeness, that sense of belonging, is to mimic each other.

Rapport is also the key to NLP. If you don't have a good rapport with someone else, you probably won't be able to connect clearly with them. You probably won't be able to ensure that you are working well with them or altering their mind. You need to create that connection somehow. This is done primarily through mirroring, a process that will involve you effectively tricking the creation of that rapport. You force the point by mimicking the other person first. When you can do that, you essentially just fool their minds into doing the same back to you. You teach them that they should be mirroring you back, so they do, and as a result, you end up creating that confidence between each other.

With the rapport built through mirroring, you can then begin to tap into the other person's subconscious mind with your movements and actions. You can make it a point to change up how you move and act so that you can take control. This is done quite simply, all things considered — it just takes four simple steps:

Listen ▸ Mirror ▸ Mimic ▸ Test

Listen Actively

Start by giving the other person your entire attention. Look at them in the eyes, listen to them and nod your head as you do — three times is the perfect amount. When you use the triple nod, as it is often referred to, you tell them that you are listening, understanding, and agreeing with them. Keep your body language open at this time and make it a point to engage carefully and openly with them. Feel that you have that connection and believe in it. The belief is what helps.

Mimic Them

Next comes shifting over to starting to mimic or mirror the other person. You do this carefully. However, if you aren't careful, you can just tip them off that you are doing it — and that can cause new problems. Instead of letting them think that you are following along ad overtly copying them, latch onto something else instead. It is often recommended that you try to match your voice to theirs — make sure that you keep their pitch, speed, and excitement. If you can do this, you will start to follow along with them, and their mind will catch onto this as well — unconsciously, they will sense that you are following along, and they will start building up that rapport.

Find Their Signature

Every person has his or her signature when they talk. It is something that is done for emphasis over the conversation. Some people have something physical—they may move in a certain way. Others may have something verbal, such as saying something that shows that they have made their point, kind of like a catchphrase. Figure out what the other person's is so that you can make good use of it. You need to know what theirs is so that you can take full advantage of the ability to create that rapport for yourself. When you have identified it, watch to see when you think that they are getting ready to use it—and then beat them to using it. They will be thrilled that you seem to be on the same page as them, and you will start-up that rapport.

Test It

Finally, the last thing for you to do is test the situation. The best way to test it is to make some small, innocuous motion and see if the other person follows along. If they do, you were probably successful. If not, you might want to try again.

Conclusion

Whether you are interested in using NLP or manipulation, reading body language, or employing hypnosis to better yourself or manipulate others; there is one characteristic that most increases your chances of success with any of the four aforementioned methods: confidence. It's really quite simple—if you don't believe in yourself, why should anybody shape their beliefs around you? Keep your confidence levels high by referring back to the postural tips and tricks in this book.

You are probably not sure how to start or where to start from in your quest to protect yourself from dark psychology. Given that the content of this book is wide, you must give yourself to learn the protection techniques one by one. A good starting place would be an in-depth understanding of NLP. As soon as you can read the thoughts of people using NLP, you will be on track to protect yourself and any person in your family from manipulation.

Anyone can learn how to work with NLP. It is not a secret that is just meant for some.

When you are ready to learn a little bit more about NLP, especially when it comes to dark NLP, make sure to use this guidebook to make sure that you get started on the right track.

Be mindful that these techniques aren't scientifically proven but have been tested and developed with experience and results over time.

Having read this book does not mean that you should not read another book about NLP Dark Psychology; information is never enough, so expanding your knowledge is always the best thing to do.

Having read the book and understood everything, you should get started. Once you have known everything about NLP Dark Psychology, you can decide how to use it for your own gains, making people do whatever you wish. The mind control, manipulation, and persuasion techniques are the ultimate deals to use for your day-to-day life; it does not have to sound like it is a wrong act to you. Having learned how to manipulate and persuade others gives you tips on how you can manage the thought process of others or become a manipulator, too.

Even if you don't want to become a manipulator or persuader yourself, you have learned about the morality and immorality of the concepts of dark psychology such as mind control, manipulation, and persuasion. If it sounds useful to you, you can apply the tactics in the various sectors discussed; in advertising, politics, in media, church, or even in school and home.

Each individual is unique in character and behavior, and this is a limitation as to how effectively each technique of NLP could work for them.

When you are in control of the techniques, you have an option to choose them wisely, depending on where, when, and for whom they are employed rather than permitting them to control your mind and thought process. Persuasion, negotiation, or manipulation cannot follow specific fixed steps or procedures to ensure their success. Instead, it could work differently depending on an assortment of variables like behavioral patterns, attitudes, circumstances, and personalities. Therefore, it is totally in your hands to discover a recipe for NLP techniques that will work successfully for you.

This book opens up your mind to the reality of the dark world in which we live. Although most people look good on the outside, there are many who plot evil against others. If you wish to protect yourself from all the dark aspects of life, you must learn to read people.